A Dog & Cat Relationship

by Majo

Illustrated by Adrienne Brown

This is the story about the relationship between a dog and a cat. You may think that's a strange combination. But, as they say, "Love is blind."

The cat loved her dog. He was very strong and handsome. She felt safe and secure around him. She knew he would always be there to protect her. Cat loved to watch Dog run fast and jump high. She felt proud of him and proud to be his wife.

The dog loved his cat. She was sleek and beautiful. She was very neat about her appearance and gentle in her ways. Those were qualities the dog lacked because of his gruffness and his rough and tumble nature. When he would lay his big shaggy head on her smooth, silky lap, listening to her purr ever so softly, he would swear he was in heaven.

2

Unlike most fairy tales… "and they lived happily ever after", this was not a fairy tale. There were some ups and downs, and a little tension here and there. Gradually, there were some arguments. Then came a few sleepless nights. Soon there were moments of doubt. Had they made a big mistake in marrying each other? It sometimes seemed that the very things that had been attractive before marriage now drove them further apart.

The dog was very gregarious and enjoyed being around his many friends. The cat was rather shy and timid and felt uncomfortable in crowds. When they would go to parties, Dog was the center of attention… telling stories and funny cat jokes. Cat, on the other hand, hoping no one would disturb her tranquility, would curl up in a corner of the crowded room.

6

At home, however, things were quite different. Cat was a flurry of activity. She cleaned and dusted and threw things out. She kept their home nice and neat. Dog liked to lie around. He only did things when Cat hissed at him. Sometimes, just when Cat was ready to put dinner on the table, Dog would run off to play with the other dogs.   This made Cat fume with anger. She would remain cold and aloof. She hoped Dog would realize why she was so upset.

Often times they would argue. "Why can't you be more like me?"
"Well, why can't you be more like me?" Round and round they would go.
The cat did not like to argue with the dog. She often found herself apologizing
for the sake of peace. "Why bother," she would think.

In spite of their problems, the dog treasured the cat and the cat cherished the dog. But even in their affection, they were opposites. The dog was warm and cuddly while the cat was cool and suspicious. Dog wanted to snuggle with the cat and feel her soft fur against his curly mane. He enjoyed the scent of her body and the sparkle of her clear, green eyes. Even though the cat loved the dog, she found it difficult to show affection. She would rather demonstrate her love by doing things to please the dog. She cooked his favorite T Bone steak. She tried to be quiet while he watched his favorite show. Sometimes she even bought a special toy for him to chew.

Many times the dog would tell the cat about his dreams for their future and how simply marvelous life was going to be. The cat could only think of today. The future made her feel worried and uncertain.

At times, the dog felt disappointed in their relationship, and even rejected by the cat. The cat, on the other hand, felt misunderstood. For both, there were times of loneliness… "This isn't the way I thought it would be. Where did we go wrong? Is this all there is to life?" But they never shared their secret thoughts and feelings with one another.

One day, as they were strolling through the woods, they got very, very lost. It was like being in a maze. Of course, each accused the other for their predicament and assumed they knew the best way out of this mess.

Night fell swiftly. The darkness engulfed them like fog rolling in off the ocean. They were totally alone and frightened.

Suddenly they heard a booming voice from above.

"Whoo! Whoo! Whoo!", it bellowed.

"Who Who, Who, are you?" barked the dog.

"I am Ozzie the owl. I am governor of this forest by night."

"And who, who, who, are you?" inquired the wise old owl.

"I am Dog and this is my wife Cat. We are lost. We can't seem to find our way out of this stupid forest."

"A dog married to a cat! What a strange combination. With all my wisdom, it never ceases to amaze me how opposites attract."

"I've often wondered that myself," muttered the cat. She was quite annoyed and blamed the dog for their plight.

"What do you mean?" Ozzie asked the cat. She didn't realize he had excellent hearing and could pick up the slightest sound.

"It's all his fault that we're in this situation", grumbled the cat. "If he hadn't gone chasing that silly bird into this dumb forest, we'd be home by now."

"Oh yeah!! Well, I was chasing that silly bird into this dumb forest for you," barked the dog. "I know how much you love birds, and I was trying to make you happy. But lately, it seems nothing I do pleases you."

"You're sooooo right," purred the cat. "I should have married a cat like myself. Then I wouldn't have to put up with all your shenanigans."
"All my shenanigans," growled the dog. "Just because I like to enjoy myself.!!! Humph! If it were up to you, I'd be a recluse with no friends and nothing to do… except fix up the house."

22

Back and forth they argued. The wise old owl just sat and listened. He didn't say a word until the dog and cat were exhausted from their "go round."

"Are you quite finished?" asked the stately owl. He was very polite and did not want to intrude on their privacy.

Timidly, they shook their heads. "Can you help us?" they asked.

"I can help you, but I'm not so sure that you two will listen." His voice was strong and deep. His eyes shown with compassion and understanding. "Do you think you could do that?"

The dog and cat seemed confused…but nodded in agreement.

The owl questioned the dog, "Do you love Cat?"

"I think I do," answered Dog. "But there are times when I feel angry at her, and then I'm not so sure. I know I want to… but sometimes I just don't know how to make her happy."

"And do you love Dog?" Ozzie asked Cat.

"At times I feel empty and drained like I just don't care anymore and it scares me", the cat whispered.

The owl was silent for a while. "Hmmm, Hmmm… AH HA!!!" he erupted. " Instead of trying to change each other… a waste of precious time if you ask me… why not celebrate your unique differences", Ozzie mused.

"Huh?…What?…" the dog and cat looked puzzled. They hesitated not knowing what Ozzie meant.

"Well, ah, I could lose some weight. And I'm kind of fussy," stammered the cat.

"Sometimes I'm loud and obnoxious," grumbled the dog.
 "I'm sloppy too," he added.

"Ah yes! Well, we all could use a little improvement," Ozzie puffed.

"But what I'm trying to say is… do you love yourself just as you are… warts and all, so to speak?"

"What kind of foolishness is that?" barked the dog.

"What does that have to do with our being lost?" Inquired Cat.

"Everything!" shouted Ozzie. "You can't begin to love one another until you get to work on loving yourselves… and, of course, understanding your differences."

"Yeah, well, I think you're cuckoo!" Yelped the dog. "You're no wise old owl. You're just a fake. I think you may have a few loose screws too. "

"Yes, but I'm not lost," laughed the owl.

"He never listens to me either," snapped the cat.

"You two are nuts," bellowed Dog.

"For once, will you just be quiet and listen?" pleaded Cat.

The dog paced up and down and back and forth… shaking his head and muttering under his breath. Finally, he slumped down beside Cat and laid his heavy head on his big paws. "You were saying," he grumbled.

"As I was saying," Ozzie teased.   "First you have to accept yourself as you are… Dog, rough and tough…Cat, cool and tender. Then you are ready to appreciate each other's differences."

 Dog and Cat stared at Ozzie in disbelief.

The owl continued, "Cat, you first loved Dog because he was so strong, because he had so many friends… and also, because he was a dreamer.   These were the qualities you thought you lacked. Dog, you were attracted to Cat because she was so gentle and shy and seemed more grounded than you… qualities you thought you lacked.

"Don't you see? Together you can be gentle… and strong. Together you can be friendly… and shy. Together you can dream… but be realistic in your dreaming. Opposites can be a blessing, not a curse. You must learn how to share and work together."

"Gee," muttered the dog. "I never thought about her helping me. I always thought I should be the strong one." Cat purred and snuggled close to Dog. "It's already working," Dog announced, as his tail began to wag happily. The wise old owl flapped his wings in joy. He loved seeing the dog and cat so excited.

"Let's go home," said Cat.

"But we are still lost," replied Dog.

"Will you help us find our way out of these woods?" the dog asked the owl.

"No," said Ozzie. "I have already shown you the way. Now you are on your own… I'm sure you'll find the right path."

The dog and cat were stunned and didn't know what to say.

"You can make it" Ozzie declared. "You have each other."

Cat looked all around her and then she said to Dog, "Follow me. I have keen eyesight at night, and I will get us home."

"I will help too," said Dog. "Although I do not see as clearly as you, I can hear for miles."

"We will get home quicker if we work together," Dog said proudly.

"Let's get going." Cat purred. Lovingly, they disappeared into the forest…side by side…each leading the way toward home.

Illustrator

Adrienne Brown was born and raised in Kansas. "So early on in my childhood I was amazed by sketching and doodling". I absolutely loved picture books. As I grew up I collected all I could. I longed to be a children's book illustrator." Most of her career was in graphic design and illustration. "You name it, I have probably drawn it."

She now resides in the Mountains of Idaho with her husband and daughter. Snuggled in the mountains and illustrating as much as possible. "I love the personal collaboration with Majo and creating her characters. Helping her wonderful stories come to life is an incredible feeling. I am truly blessed to be a part of it all."

Contact Adrienne at adbrown14@gmail.com or papermoonco.com

Author Biography

Majo is a wife, mother, grandmother, writer and entrepreneur who promotes positive thinking, and achieving a high quality of life. While raising her family, she began her career as a corporate consultant, training employees in team building, sales and diversity. She also earned a real estate license, wrote a column called "The Family Hour" for a Philadelphia area newspaper and modeled in print and television. She founded three businesses to foster personal accountability, successful parenting and improving the prevalent cultural mindset regarding women in advertising.

Of all her many accomplishments, Majo is most proud of being the Mother of her eight children and grandmother of many. Majo is a beautiful, energetic and determined entrepreneur. She has written six books for children as well as adults. The first five, HUMBLE PIE, THE COOL CHAMELEON, CLEO THE COLD FISH, LESSONS ON FLYING, and A DOG AND CAT RELATIONSHIP are now available. THE DRAB CATTERPILLAR will be obtainable in the near future. It has taken her 30 years and many, many rejection letters to achieve this goal. The saying "It's never too late" and Bob Dylan's quote "He who is not busy being born, is busy dying" motivate Majo to keep growing.

Majo is married and lives in Doylestown, PA.

Contact Majo at her website:
MajoTheAuthor.com or email: mjbgd@aol.com

Made in the USA
Middletown, DE
12 January 2019